HUMAN IMPACT ON EARTH: CAUSE AND EFFECT

CHANGING COASTLINE ENVIRONMENTS

JENNA TOLLI

PowerKiDS press

New York

Published in 2020 by The Rosen Publishing Group, Inc.
29 East 21st Street, New York, NY 10010

First Edition

Editor: Jane Katirgis
Book Design: Reann Nye

Photo Credits: Series art Xiebiyun/Shutterstock.com; Alexander Tolstykh/Shutterstock.com; Cafe Racer/Shutterstock.com; cover Andrew Mayovskyy/Shutterstock.com; p. 5 Arjuna Ravikumar/500px Prime/Getty Images; p. 6 Romrodphoto/Shutterstock.com; p. 7 Romiana Lee/Shutterstock.com; p. 8 dkingsleyfish/Shutterstock.com; p. 9 ThomBal/Shutterstock.com; p.10 nik wheeler/Moment/Getty Images; p. 11 randydellinger/iStock/Getty Images Plus/Getty Images; p. 13 Paul Brennan/Shutterstock.com; p. 14 trekandshoot/Shutterstock.com; p. 15 (background) wildestanimal/Shutterstock.com; p. 15 (starfish) photobeps/Shutterstock.com; p. 16 (turtle) Benjamin Albiach Galan/Shutterstock.com; p. 16 (sign) mariakraynova/Shutterstock.com; p. 17 Photography by Mangiwau/Moment/Getty Images; p. 18 GlOck/Shutterstock.com; p. 19 Elizaveta Galitckaia/Shutterstock.com; p. 21 Maridav/Shutterstock.com; p. 22 Serenethos/Shutterstock.com; p. 23 Felix Lipov/Shutterstock.com; p. 25 DigitalGlobe/Getty Images; p. 27 Mark Wilson/Getty Images News/Getty Images; p. 28 Brooks Kraft/Corbis Historical/Getty Images; p. 29 Steve Heap/Shutterstock.com.

Cataloging-in-Publication Data

Names: Tolli, Jenna.
Title: Changing coastline environments / Jenna Tolli.
Description: New York : PowerKids Press, 2020. | Series: Human impact on Earth: cause and effect | Includes glossary and index.
Identifiers: ISBN 9781725300163 (pbk.) | ISBN 9781725300187 (library bound) | ISBN 9781725300170 (6pack)
Subjects: LCSH: Coastal ecology–Juvenile literature. | Coasts–Juvenile literature. | Coast changes–Juvenile literature.
Classification: LCC QH541.5.C65 T65 2020 | DDC 551.45'7–dc23

Manufactured in the United States of America

CPSIA Compliance Information: Batch #CSPK19. For Further Information contact Rosen Publishing, New York, New York at 1-800-237-9932.

CONTENTS

IMPORTANT IMPACTS

Have you ever built a sand castle only to find, moments later, the water has washed it away? This is just one example of how the coast is always changing.

The coast is where sea meets land. Coastlines are the outer edges, or boundaries, where these two places come together. These environments are constantly changing. Sometimes we can see small changes happen right in front of us, like when grains of sand move away with the tide on a beach. Other coastal changes can take many years to make a noticeable difference. Earth's processes change the shape of our coasts and affect the people, animals, and plants that live there. At the same time, humans also make changes to coastal environments, whether they mean to or not.

IMPACT FACTS

Coastlines are irregular and constantly changing, so they can be difficult to measure. According to some measurements, there are about 221,208 miles (356,000 km) of coastline throughout the world.

Alaska has the longest coastline in the United States. It's about 6,640 miles (10,686 km) long!

TYPES OF COASTLINES

Many people think of coastlines as sandy beaches. Beaches are made up of small particles, like grains of sand or pebbles. When seawater and wind wear away at the land, they break up rocks and minerals into tiny pieces. This process forms sand. The sand we see on a beach has been broken down over time and could have traveled many miles before it reached the shore.

COASTAL WETLANDS

Marshes and swamps are examples of wetlands. Coastal wetlands are places along the coastline where the land is full of water, or saturated. They can form near rivers and bays in places that do not drain water well. Coastal wetlands are important habitats for fish, birds, and other wildlife. The wetlands help clean water and control flooding, too.

There are rocky shores throughout the United States. For example, Acadia National Park in Maine has over 40 miles (64 km) of rocky shoreline.

There are other types of coasts, too. Rocky coastlines are formed when waves pound away at solid land. This can form cliffs. Animals that live on rocky coasts need to protect themselves from the strong waves that crash against the shore. For example, crabs and other sea animals can hide in the cracks between rocks to stay safe.

SMALL CHANGES EVERY DAY

Like most landforms on Earth, coastlines are shaped and reshaped by forces called weathering and **erosion**. Weathering is when rocks or minerals get broken down into smaller pieces. Waves and ocean winds wear them down to form a material called sediment. After the rocks are broken down by weathering, the process of erosion **transports** them to another place. Together, both of these processes change the shape of coastlines.

Coasts can change shape over different seasons, too. Storm winds can move sand away from the beach in the winter, and then waves bring it back during the summer.

Coastlines can be categorized by the forces that have shaped them. Were they mostly shaped by erosion, when land wears down and is carried away? Or did they form by deposition, when sediment builds up to create landforms? Rocky coasts with cliffs are shaped by erosion, but sandy beaches are shaped by deposition of sediment.

BIG CHANGES OVER TIME

Over time, processes such as weathering and erosion change the shape of coastlines. Erosion can cause beaches to get narrower. When there is less sand between the ocean and the land, buildings on the coast are at risk. This is because the beach and sand dunes protect things behind them from wind and waves.

Homes on the California coast between Ventura and Santa Barbara are built directly on the coastline. They are at risk from erosion.

IMPACT FACTS

Coastline erosion is very expensive. Each year, it causes approximately $500 million in building damage and loss of land in the United States.

CLIFF RETREAT

Erosion can put buildings on cliffs in danger. When a lighthouse named Southeast Light was built in 1875 on Block Island, Rhode Island, it was more than 300 feet (91 m) from the edge of a cliff. Erosion caused land on the cliff to **retreat** and fall over time, and the distance to the ocean went down to only 55 feet (17 m) over 115 years. In 1993, the lighthouse was moved farther back to keep it safe.

Coastal erosion can also cause destruction on cliffs, such as landslides. When waves push against land, the base of a cliff gets eroded and forms a notch, or indent, at the bottom. This makes the cliff steeper. As the sediment gets removed over time, the cliff can become **unstable.** Pieces of the coast can break and fall into the water.

STORM THREATS

Weathering and erosion are always happening, but they happen on a much bigger scale during **tropical storms**. Storms such as hurricanes and tsunamis can make major changes to coastal environments very quickly. Hurricanes are large storms that form over the water and have high-speed winds. When hurricanes make **landfall**, they can cause a lot of destruction to environments, houses, and communities.

Storm surge is a change in water level that is caused by one of these storms. This can cause water levels to rise more than 20 feet (6 m) higher than normal. The water floods communities. It causes a lot of destruction, from beach erosion on the coast to damage to coastal roads and buildings.

IMPACT FACTS

Storms can also cause new inlets to form on coasts. Inlets are narrow passageways that connect one body of water to another.

In 2017, Hurricane Irma impacted the United States and other countries. The waves and storm surge caused significant damage and erosion to the coast.

13

LIVING ALONG THE COAST

Almost 40 percent of people in the United States live on or near a coastline. Many of the biggest cities around the world are located on coasts, too. Considering the risks that people who live on coasts face, why do so many people choose to call the coast home?

Throughout history, cities have been built on coasts near ports, which is where boats can load and unload goods or passengers. These areas on the coast make trade and transportation easier using water travel. Many people also travel to beaches to visit, which makes tourism important for these areas. Overall, coastal areas provide job opportunities and access to resources, which make them very popular places to live.

One of the largest ports in the United States is in Long Beach, California.

HOME TO MANY

There are a lot of marine plants and animals that live on coastlines too, such as crabs, sea stars, sea turtles, and many more. Beach grass also grows on certain parts of the coast. Plants can help to keep sand dunes in one place by protecting them from wind.

SEA STARS

IMPACT FACTS

Did you know that coral reefs help to protect our coasts? They act as barriers to prevent damage from strong waves and storms that might otherwise hit the shore.

COASTAL DEVELOPMENT

Throughout history, humans have made changes to the environment to help them **thrive** on Earth. Some of these activities have had negative effects on the planet, including Earth's oceans and coastlines. Because coasts are such a popular place to visit and live, people have built more roads, houses, and hotels there over time. This can make beaches crowded and narrower. It can also change natural processes that happen on the coast, such as how tides come to shore and how sediment moves along the beach.

Loggerhead sea turtles build nests and lay eggs on certain coasts. They can be threatened by human activity and coastal development. Areas of some beaches are protected to help keep the turtles and their nesting areas safe.

DO NOT DISTURB
SEA TURTLE
NEST
VIOLATORS SUBJECT
TO FINES AND
IMPRISONMENT

BARRIER ISLANDS

Barrier islands are long, sandy islands that are parallel to the main coast. These islands help to protect the mainland from the effects of storms and flooding caused by the ocean. Barrier islands are popular places for vacations and beach homes, and a lot of coastal development takes place there.

Development on the coast can also change the environments of the plants and animals that live there. When new structures are built, it disturbs natural habitats or takes them away completely.

EFFECTS OF POLLUTION

Humans also contribute to marine pollution, which affects oceans, coastlines, and wildlife. Most of the pollution we see in the ocean actually starts on land. When waste is not disposed of properly, it can make its way to oceans. Then the waves and currents can make it wash up on the shore. Things like plastic, cans, and other garbage get pushed to the shore and can harm animals that live there.

Sewage and chemical waste also pollute our oceans and coasts. When oil is spilled into the water, the wind can push it to the shore, too. Oil is poisonous and can harm or kill animals if they consume it. It can also cover their fur or feathers, which makes it harder for them to stay warm.

We can do our part to prevent pollution by picking up after ourselves when we visit coastlines. It's also important to be aware of the negative effects that building near coastlines can have.

GLOBAL CHANGES

Climate change is when a place's regular weather patterns start to change. This can result in a change to a location's usual temperature for the season. Or it might mean a change in the amount of rain per year.

Scientists have shown that Earth's climate is about 1°F (0.6°C) warmer than it was 100 years ago. Earth's warming climate melts some glaciers and ice in cold parts of the planet. More water gets released into places where it wasn't before, which causes ocean levels to slowly rise. When these levels get higher, the erosion on coasts moves faster.

Higher sea levels mean more flooding in coastal areas. Not only can this cause significant damage to beaches and islands themselves, it is also a threat for the people, plants, and animals that live near them.

Some glaciers in parts of
Alaska are melting faster today
than they have in 400 years.

CLIMATE CHANGE IMPACTS

As the temperature on Earth continues to get warmer, there will be more
extreme weather changes and stronger storms in the future. We have
started to see some of these changes already. Research has shown that
human activities, such as burning **fossil fuels**, have contributed to the
climate changes we are seeing today. One way to reduce human impact is
by using clean and efficient energy sources, such as solar and wind power.

REACTING TO NATURE

People are constantly looking for ways to prevent damage caused by forces in nature. For the millions of people who live near coasts, this is especially important. Sometimes these protections help one part of the coast but might cause damage to another area. These changes can also **interfere** with natural processes of the coast.

There are also more natural options to help protect coastal areas. For example, extra sand can be added to existing sand dunes on beaches to protect them. This is called beach replenishment.

Seawalls are one example of this. These structures are used to stop sand from being swept away by the tide. While seawalls might help erosion in one area, they can actually leave other parts of the beach without sand. When waves hit the seawall instead of sand on a beach, the waves can go back to the ocean with more energy. This can make the beach in front of them erode even faster.

MEASURING COASTAL CHANGE

How do we know that coastlines are changing? We can see some of the small changes on our own, like when tides move sand away from beaches. To see changes on a bigger scale, we can use photos and satellite images from different time periods. By looking at the same area at different times, we can see how coastal areas have changed over many years, or even after one large storm. Satellites are also used to track when storms are coming and when people near the coast need to **evacuate** to stay safe.

Scientists can also use information from the past to measure changes. For example, they can compare the heights of sand dunes before and after a storm. These measurements help scientists **estimate** how much damage was caused to areas of the beach.

These are satellite images of New Orleans, Louisiana, before and after Hurricane Katrina hit the area in 2005. >

BEFORE
HURRICANE KATRINA

AFTER
HURRICANE KATRINA

25

There are a number of government agencies and programs that study Earth and its different processes. Each agency and department has an important role in protecting people's safety, the environment, and Earth's natural resources. They measure things such as environmental changes and threats to coastal communities. Each agency has a specific mission and different **initiatives**.

For example, the mission of the United States Environmental Protection Agency (EPA) is "to protect human health and the environment." When studies showed that parts of the country were losing thousands of acres of coastal wetlands over the years, the EPA created the Coastal Wetlands Initiative. Goals of this initiative are to understand the threats to coastal wetlands and find ways to better protect them.

IMPACT FACTS

The National Oceanic and Atmospheric Administration (NOAA) Marine **Debris** Program helps to educate the public about the harm of marine debris. The program also researches impacts and solutions for prevention and supports local debris removal projects.

NOAA's National Weather Service tracks weather and water changes. They notify the public when it is not safe to be on the coast or near the ocean due to bad weather or high winds.

PROTECTING OUR PLANET

The EPA was created in 1970 when Richard Nixon was president. In the 1960s, it became clear that pollution and other environmental problems were harming our planet. For example, air pollution was such a problem that it could be hard to breathe in certain places. Nixon and his administration decided more needed to be done. The EPA was formed to make sure the environment and our resources would be protected.

We can't change what nature will throw at us, but we can use science and history to help protect ourselves and our environment from negative effects. One way to keep ourselves safe is to build houses on the coastlines to **withstand** storms better. This can include things like building homes on stilts, placing strong shutters on windows to shield them from high-speed winds, and adding doors that prevent leaks.

When visiting a coast, it is important to leave areas the way we find them. For example, we can prevent damage to sand dunes by obeying signs on the beach for areas where we shouldn't walk. Sand dunes not only help to reduce erosion on the coast, but they are also home to many plants and animals.

ENVIRONMENTALLY SENSITIVE AREA

PLEASE STAY OFF THE DUNES

Cities at risk of coastal flooding have websites to help residents protect their homes and land. These houses in Malibu, California, are raised on stilts to protect them from flooding.

REDUCING OUR IMPACT

Throughout history, we have seen many different ways nature can change our coastlines. This list includes coastal erosion, damage from storms, and climate change, which are all still happening today. Humans have also been the cause of some of the changes we see on our coastlines through coastal development, human-made climate change, and pollution.

Although human civilizations may always have negative impacts on the environment, there are still ways we can conserve our resources and limit these effects in the future. As we learn more about how climate change threatens our coastlines, environmental agencies can help to protect them by changing laws and policies. By limiting pollution and reducing waste, everyone can do their part to help protect our coastal environments and coastline communities.

GLOSSARY

debris: Scattered pieces of garbage or waste.

erosion: The wearing away of the earth's surface by wind or water.

estimate: To judge the approximate amount.

evacuate: To leave a place of danger.

fossil fuels: A fuel formed from the remains of dead plants and animals.

initiative: Taking the first step to solve a problem.

interfere: To stop or to make slower.

landfall: Reaching the land.

retreat: To move back.

thrive: To grow successfully.

transport: To move something from one place to another.

tropical storm: A very strong wind system that forms over a tropical ocean.

unstable: Changing unpredictably.

withstand: To stand up against something and avoid being damaged.

WEBSITES

Due to the changing nature of Internet links, PowerKids Press has developed an online list of websites related to the subject of this book. This site is updated regularly. Please use this link to access the list: www.powerkidslinks.com/HIOE/coast